In Case of Sudden Free Fall

Deborah Bogen

Cover & interior design: Daniel Krawiec

ISBN 978-0-936481-17-3
Library of Congress Control Number: 2017951044

Jacar Press
6617 Deerview Trail
Durham, NC 27712
www.jacarpress.com

Acknowledgments

I am grateful to the editors who published the following poems (some under different names):

The Gettysburg Review: Me and Dickens; In the Arboretum

Vox Populi: In English We Call This Heaven; Rue Saint-Séverin; For the Girl Who Came to Class With Her Altered Body; Studying Stalin and Shostakovich

Offcourse: In Praise of What Remains Unfinished; Me and Vincent; To Tell a Story

New Letters: My Stint as a Librarian; The Year God Discovered Pointillism; How-to for the Daughters of Suicides; Adam Boots, Progenitor; The Year God Developed Cataracts; Off-Broadway Free Fall. These poems also won the New Letters Poetry Prize for 2016

One (More) Glass: Addiction

Poetry Daily featured The Year God Developed Cataracts 5/16/17

Contents

for Lynn
dear sister, dear midwife, dear conspirator

To Tell a Story

There's no secret to syntax. The crown rusts. The peasants sharpen their pikes. A carriage comes secretly through the forest. There's a distant bell and suddenly the trees are dancing fire. Over there a road leads off to paradise but crossing the mountains is perilous and here, in the middle of the story, we find a girl who sits patiently in the presence of a great love. In the square, flower sellers sell flowers. Patrons and fortune-tellers quarrel among themselves. The crown remains unclaimed, but a clock is ticking and in the bishop's cellar a small child holds his breath. Near the end a young man stands up. There's always one of these. He picks up the crown and says, "My mouth is full of God."

In the Arboretum

This is not the age for angels with lances, he said. Plant your feet. Then lean and arrive. Swing your arms as if you are pregnant and getting off a bus in the wrong town. Swing your arms to number your plagues. Your arms are your perished sisters. Your arms are your broken mother. Surrender to this narrowing of possible joys.

Let your tongue fall into its ditch and be grateful for the unbidden words circling your skull. They are your crown. They will allow you to stay in the room. The room of the heavens, or if you prefer the room of the forest. If the breath becomes confused, re-plant your feet. You belong in this room. Here, where every sigh is a safety valve. Turn your brain on, he said, but barely.

In English We Call This Heaven

If solace for this long tired war comes with sky, if it is here now, beside us, behind us, and there above. Who holds the tarnished mirror that curves over fields flush with bloodied pawns, broken and soon for the box? And if it is truly sky beneath which we do our constant winnowing, under which we point crying chaff! chaff! chaff! why do we not look up?

Winter raises his axe. We cross wet fields, wary, still seeking sustenance and succor. Light. And light. Wanting what's after aftermath, perhaps a vault in which moon and stars...

Me and Dickens

I used to dream in bird language. Everything sound and feathers, but now it's winter. You can't find many birds. The snow's stained with soot and along the boulevard the houses of rich men broadcast a blonde electric glow. It's tranquil, but I miss the birds, the cheerful lunatic birds. The flutey yellow ones, and the ones shaped like green guitars.

Dickens said it. All partings foreshadow. And now the birds are gone. The birds have flown away. But I'm still here. Like Charlie, I ramble, drawn to the windows of other people's houses where golden-haired children practice their green violins.

Translation as Lightning Rod

At the reading the woman raises both hands. She's signing a large hello, a halo of symbols and consonants. Her hands are wavering birds, then staccato castanets. They turn and tumble, first waterfall, then angry drum. The air trembles as she calls down an avalanche, a tempest of translation. Poems. Reborn in every gesture.

And what does it matter if she "gets it right?" Mistake, seen from another angle, may ignite new dream windows, some oddly Russian and deep with snow.

I Thought He Said

there's healing in the experience of awe. Be an aspen quaking. So I got out my old notebooks and read everything I once believed. Oh God of My Misunderstanding, there is nothing trustworthy in my house. The world blossoms into secrecy and complexity while at the Apple Store geniuses work bestowing new passwords. Their shirts are the color of night sky just before the stars appear, here, in the hospital waiting room.

Master Class

Dear mentor, dear stranger, I am attracted to your apparatus, to your breathing (so like prayer) and your vivid death imagery. But dear companion, dear exemplar, what if my breath becomes confused? What if I can't lift the crowbar that opens boxed hearts?

Is it enough to leave geraniums on the stairs to heaven? To traffic in symbols and colloquy? Part of me longs to snake carelessly into town, poised and accomplished, but another part loves the wild beauty of free fall. Dear counselor, dear conspirator, I'm still down here in the cellar, my teeth stained by bitter fruit, my hand sunk deep where it does not belong.

For the Returned

They stand at the door, gray stains in the air, and we ache to mend them. To touch them, to kiss them back from the dead. We do not want to turn our backs, these hips and thighs, but tell us, you generals, how do we cherish those who are neither hot nor cold?

Look. The children shy away. The dogs watch warily. Even the horses, wild once themselves, busy their gaze with the field.

Me and Sartre

Here's a tip from Jean-Paul: it's time to abandon the ancients. We don't need their golden temples, their rituals, their apocalyptic prophecies. Every day the sun rises like a guillotine. It looks down on *our* gods — forged from money and blood. They're hungry, our gods. They want to eat. Their minions run around tricked out in vests and detonators.

There's no poetry in that, no myth-heavy sacrament — still, I think Sartre got it right: *There may be more beautiful times, but this one is ours.*

Off Broadway Free Fall

The restaurant's an aquarium. We're tethered to our ta-
ble, mumbling over the script. The barkeep hums, glass-
es clink — but otherwise it's a tomb. In this black and
white production of the Lunch Game you play the part
of the out-of-towner. Formerly the love interest, I'm now
the comic foil, attracted to men with money but appalled
at the way they made it. Waiters in pointed shoes saun-
ter by hoping to impress a director. A parade of priests
shows up stage right. Black robes. Silver crosses. They
look, don't you think, like extras from *Zorro*, that new
one, where vampires were hammered into the script.

Jazz

We carry. We carry it, alter and vary it, receive and ache
till we're tranced by it, swallowing sound till we're pierced
by the lance, moved by it, grooved by the carrying angels
who slide with the bone of it, re-work the stone of it, suf-
fer the bright holy pain of it, reamed by the strain of the
horn, mauled with it, all of it, crawl with it right to the lip
of the pit, and we haul all the joy of it, witness the swing
of the axe splitting air as we hail the new and the late of
it, marking our souls, if it's souls we got, bringing our
own to it, forced by the deep and the singular want of it,
beat of it, struggle and rip of it, caught, we carry the hip
of it, fury and stick of it, wild rack and trip of it, we all,
we carry. We praise and we carry it.

Singing into the Void

Dear My Dead. They say there's no speed-of-sound in space. So that's probably true in heaven. And in nirvana. And in paradise. It's probably as quiet as mist with not a whisper or jingle to signal you're *there*.

And what's left for the living is a gap. Between your face and memory. Between words and what we mean. Between whatever motors this world and everything else. Only wind truly connects. Connects me to your updraft. Above me invisible jets cut across the heavens. If I could only find the number, I bet I could call you up.

Studying Stalin and Shostakovich

History's a country of rubble and supposing. We've thrown things into the air that will never touch the ground. It's hard to know what's going on, but you can be sure of one thing: there's always a man with a gun.

When Tukhachevsky was shot, they say that's when Dmitri wrote his great lament. They mean that's *why* he wrote it. They love that orderly A caused B. But lately I've been thinking about a pack of dogs let loose on the mesa.

The Year God Developed Cataracts

the clouds erupted — slate grey, charcoal. Almost black.
Winds shredded sky, water cut skin, so Turner knew he
had no choice. He chartered a ship, then tied himself to
the mast to see for himself.

Eventually even Monet changed his paints, the world first
yellow-casted, then blue, then a miraculous red. Thus it
was strangely real. As vision itself is too much too soon
too fast too full too bright too loud too hot too close —
like fainting, but before you black out.

Trouble in Mind

I want to tell you. But my mouth's a stone turned inside out.

That's how thoughts alter flesh. They fill your head with bees, turn a good throat didgeridoo. And this thing I want to say...it's not even a secret. Just oddly coded, a one-time-liminal-demonstration of *elusive* + *random*.

That's why I ache to give it weight. To master what's unfolding in my brain. I open my mouth.

But.

Looking at *Guernica*

I'm thinking in terms of stage props, rubber knives and
plausible explanations. You say I should relax, take an as-
pirin, make some coffee, but where-oh-where, old friend,
are the shield-walls for our hearts? These days, these ter-
rible days, you tell me are only warnings, but we've both
seen *Guernica*. Chaos is a wild-eyed bull standing over a
dead child and Christians or no-Christians the messiah
isn't coming.

So we walk to the cemetery, to look at all the old-timey
names on the monuments. Did you know, I say, that *in-
scribed* is just another word for cut?

Me and Vincent

Van Gogh painted moths. It's rarely mentioned, but he did. And when he was crumbling, unhinged by *too-much-nature*, he drew caterpillars and broken leaves, dimming the world to see if he could stay.

Vincent, I hope you know the road menders are still at work. And in the poets' garden and the garden of the asylum ravens continue to frank the air. I think of you there, standing at the window while stars churned the sky to a throbbing canvas. And the winds were brazen, weren't they? So demanding, so bright-edged with gold. It was all too much, Vincent. Too much.

How I Did Not Become a Painter

Jeff looks at a vase, then paints a pilfered sky. He paints leaves as interruptions and burly bovine anchors, and when he does we're moved to match our math to his equation, to dream we too are painters, the way the leaves dream they're feathers.

Child-me understood the night. In its darkness I flew above the neighborhoods, unburdened and in love with whatever motors this world. That flying was my worship. That flying was my art. Till someone shook me. Said, wake up. Said, sit up straight. Said, don't look into the dark. So I did not look. Then I did not look again.

Museum Talk

In this painting a forest of arms lifts to toast you. In this painting snow flaunts itself in ever-larger drifts. And here's a landscape severed by storms where valets are rushing to park the frozen cars. This one portrays your heart as a city of secret staircases. And in this one, it's a bird with a broken beak. Remember when we used to sleep entwined, sister? The long nights we mourned. In this painting I'm left standing by the water. There's a murmured collage of voices.

Rue Saint-Séverin

Dirt and hunger. Foreheads burnt, no, branded by heat.
Backpacks. Paper cups. Bundles that are everything we
own. Beneath the gargoyles, our babies sleep.

We used to have houses. Once we had windows. Now we
live at the edge of the world where sometimes at night the
Shade lifts his blade. Still, we must rest. We must sleep.
We turn away, tucking ourselves into our skin, ignoring
the feet that pass.

And no one stops. No one says *these stones are not pillows.*
What prophecy hides in the blur of our breathing? Some-
thing is here. And something is coming.

The News from Japan is Light and Multisyllabic

After a death we need a to-do list. The man from the cemetery wants a deposit. There're things to pick up from the dry cleaners. Even tying your shoes stops you thinking *match flame, moth wing.*

And because death is the stone we take into the body, we find ourselves resurrecting girlish love songs. We get up in the middle of the night to make butter and sugar sandwiches and listen to radio stations from far away. And we are not to be admonished. And we are not to be blamed. We have seen the welded crosses, twisted and tossed out behind the caretaker's shed.

Addiction

Somewhere in the Rockies a girl with hair the color of
lotus blossoms steals clean white sheets from her grand-
mother's clothesline. Granny doesn't notice. She's busy
sipping Smirnoff and watching Wyoming's theatrical
ether gild the mountains. Undone by all that glory Gran-
ny dies. But her hunger doesn't. It streams to the girl-
become-woman who reforms. Stops stealing. Becomes a
painter with lotus-colored hair.

Her paintings sell. She's almost famous, but fame brings
no relief. She's still at it, slave to the craving, strung out
on light's ever-shifting tessellations. While you're reading
this — I mean right now — she's out there in Wyoming,
layering titanium and zinc onto another canvas. She's
gripping the knife, gritting her teeth...

Peeking through the Keyhole at the Bride

The ring and the dress: gestures in the direction of a marriage. Because we were a first try, a rough sketch, a dress rehearsal. And it's true — we flopped, but let's not feed the drama. Nobody died. The babies crawled into robust bodies, pulled themselves up and took to running around. There were soccer games. Barbecues. Christmases. Halloween. And yes, a wind that blew through us. I kept the coffee maker. You took the guitar. The piano was mine. You needed the truck. And just like that we were done, but I can still recall waking in the middle of the night, afraid of what my hands might do.

The Year God Discovered Pointillism

winter wouldn't quit. There was a generalized, harmonized breathing, but no speech, no words, as if talk had never been real. We grew attentive to small changes, spatial ones and even vacillating pressures. Some days we tasted stillness, but it was nothing mystical. It was only weather.

This is not meant to confuse you. Think of snow-softened edges, contrasts smudged — hushed, the way mother hushed your questions without even speaking. It was the snow in her that stopped your breath and filled the room with glitter.

Adam Boots, Progenitor

Noting the Certainty and Uncertainty of Death Adam Boots willed away his sorrel mare and bed and blanket. Weak, and also Sick, but of Perfect Mind and Memory, he granted to his son a saddle five years old. He was Lutheran, prepared to go whenever it pleased his God to call — and having left a parcel of land lying in and being in the county of Delaware in the state of Indiana, he committed his flesh freely unto the earth, certain he would receive it back at the general resurrection. This one sheet of paper, my great-great-grandfather's will, has a seal at the bottom. He had his friend, Jonathan Ketterman, and his other friend, David, who may have been a Jew, swear it was all true, all Adam, with his broken body and his Perfect Mind.

For the Girl Who Came to Class with Her Altered Body

Preferring comfort, you plan to discard your powers.
To bury them in the garden or in your neighbor's field. I
don't blame you. You're tired of the chronic shivers, worn
out by the way art's part cotton candy, part crucifixion.

But if you've learned to love a splintery music only you
can hear you will go back. You'll dig them up. What you're
craving might be as close as friendly fire or as distant as
Tibet. But in the end you must trust the tongue's strange
instincts. It's that lonely here. And we have so much time.

Dream Where I'm Riding a Bus

We're enclosed in aluminum that's pimped out in sunset-smolder. The driver delivers a steady stream of knock-knock jokes, but my mind's glued to the visuals. The chaos. And the heat. Los Angeles is glorious the way a firestorm is glorious. And me? I'm a fetus awash in the blood of the Lamb. Born pilgrim, I'm marked by cinder smudge and tire track, but in this dream I do not mind the haze. I do not fear the guillotine. At last the prophecy has been fulfilled: *And under every overpass, an encampment of the chosen.*

Literary Gossip

Come on. You can tell me. Who's just been asylumed and who's articulating essential insight? Who's hung up on elegant semantics and who's reporting the news under anesthesia? Which one's in debt to the devil, or staining the page with rusty blood? I'm looking for some liter- ary chinwag 'cause lately I've lost my own music and I need a little something to shake things loose. So tell me, sweet sister, whose ruptured heart is a storefront church? Amongst us all, who's the most successful vulture?

All Afternoon You Think of Heat and Dirt and Dancing

while you wait for the man with the leaf blower to stop. You want the washer to quit gnashing its teeth. The dryer to catch its breath. You're against the water moving through the hoses although it only means to make up for the sun whose gaze is killing the grass, and also us, but more slowly.

You know a secret but what can you do, you with your religion, your medication, your pricey threads and fresh tattoos? There's a noise that is not quite breathing. There are eyes cut from cardboard in the alley. There's a card in your wallet with a number you can call, but everyday the sun rises like a guillotine. You watch the ants march into the shade of your mini-van.

Dream in Which Sky Makes it Real

I couldn't fit the egg in the apple, or the apple in the stone.
I couldn't keep the bird with the broken beak. She was a
wild sweep of wings, a flash of frantic red, lofting, then
falling, then climbing again. She kept flying, pummeling
the Rapture with her small soft body. Her soft red body.
Some say a dream of the dead means water. Some say it's
money in your mouth.

The Fourth Bowl of Wrath

For a time it was only windy, as if a storm approached.
Then dervishes in trees. Gusts that cut skin, that spit un-
tethered earth till rocks were arrows. Sparrows and even
the chickens left us. And water? It was moody. Unlikely.
Finally not-at-all.

Thus we came to understand the Fourth Bowl of Wrath,
God's blistering breath on the land. Heaven was a bug-
thickened bruised catastrophe under which cows sick-
ened. Kids sickened. Diggers begged pardon as grit hit
coffins. And every day, the sun rose like a guillotine.

My Stint as a Librarian

The aquarium's alive with yellow angelfish directing peo-
ple to the children's section. Little lamps as bright as shot
glasses mark the darkened hall.

In one corner a father reads his boy a book about the
moon. *The moon,* I interject, *is a poetic object upon which
men have golfed.* At my desk a woman surrenders the
books her daughter borrowed. The girl died last week.
The woman says she's making plans to strike out on her
own. To swim the Atlantic.

This building was built stone by stone. Minerals and earth,
I tell her, but she is already far away, listening to some old
song. The record keeps skipping in the same place, the
same place, the same place.

Late Night Free Fall

It's dark, so we see with our hands, with our skin, with
the skin of our bellies and breasts, and our rumps — how
they rumple the sheets. We meet in this bed and open
our hands, and the eyes of our hands. We flutter their
lashes and send them deep into valleys, over cambers and
arches, teaching them *see* and *breathe* and *behold*. We
abandon, grow voluptuous, learning *witness* and *feast*,
our bodies born to be touched, to be burrowed into, to
be lit only by sparks, the sparks that leap from our hands
with their eyes, and their marvelous lashes.

Heavy Rains Produce Flood Conditions

without warning the radio said. So it was too late to get out. That made God a hot topic. *Forget the body's sorry-ass shelf life,* Dick told us. *The Blessed Lord can make all grace abound.*

We passed a bottle. Six humans huddled on a desert, flat up against maelstrom and indefinite night. We took to singing, drank some more, told our worn-out stories. We didn't look like much, but we never flinched. We didn't cower. That night we glorified our own lives. And that's when the yowling winds, they came for us.

Free Fall

Imagine falling safely into everything: a creek spit-shining stones; anxiety and affluence cheek-to-cheek on Wall Street; the scarred retina that has become a treasured blind spot. Imagine falling through Earth-time to redwood-time to you. Somewhere on that journey you'll notice that the laws of physics function mainly as myth — but if you lay your head on your lover's chest, you can hear the world's blossoming quantified.

Avery Parrish as Prophet

Here's the question: when Avery Parrish wrote *After Hours* did he know what he was doing? Did he think it could undo the car crash, erase late night bar fights? Who was it he meant to save? And did he think about my news-shredded soul sinking into his sounds or about some jazz-starved Jewish kid smuggling a radio into bed at night, stashing it under the covers so he could listen to Sonny Rollins and Sonny Stitt make things right?

Me and Baudelaire

It's a ritual. Every year. To greet Baudelaire. I return to the city. Enter the gates where time dissolves.

Filtered light, the paths swept clean. And a stillness that should soothe, but the miniature barbicans disquiet. Embryonic grasses seethe beneath remnants of cigarettes, metro tickets, dead flowers. No matter — this is the month Baudelaire stirs. He turns, rousting Beckett. Dreyfus. Soutine.

At least Sartre & Simone lay still, shunning the narrow houses where Christians continue to torment their god. But in truth, everything is brutal here. Broken windows. Broken stone. Even my Baudelaire who has at last come finally, and cruelly, between his mother and her general.

Dream in Which I Cannot Find the Baby

The baby's shoes are tied together. They hang around my neck. I stand beneath the oak tree where an empty swing sways. There's someone I should call for help, but in the dream I don't believe in numbers. The fives are all esses and I'm having a problem with grammar. I am pretty having trouble with words that want order. It might be you I should call, but where's your sentence? And who stole the soggy phone book? I wake to crying and my milk comes down.

To the Girl Who's Up Late Reading the History of the World and has made it to the Assyrians

Because the body's truth is not eternal, and we are never wholly arrived, you must choose how you will spend your days. There's much to value in rubble, but you can waste a lifetime bent over, picking through shards. Meanwhile, the moon is waiting. So sink your teeth into it. It will flood your mouth with moon juice. And a single blade of grass, one stalk sweet and sharp can mark your tongue with fire. Someday a hard-ass snow will blow you path-less. That's when you'll learn the left hand has everything to teach you. Consider baptism by lilac scent. And re-member — there's always someone you're about to meet.

Spit-shining My Soul

Water seeps through the drainpipe ahead of the season. It has no interest in rebirth. This is how I am, I think. Unstrung. Peeking through keyholes, needing a way to put Michael in past tense. To stop wondering if he dreams colors there.

Some days my heart's a storefront church where everybody's saved. Sometimes Bad Mary turns in my sleep. I don't think of him every day, but this morning I watched a plane rise to its own applause on silvery runways of air.

Naming the Necessary Wasted Years

One stone gone tomb, wind-honed she went, one heart
gone bone, stunned song, dumb-toned, no loon, no hand,
no child, spent moan, deep pond, her song a vague half-
tone. This seam unsewn, undone, unmeant, the heart
gone sour, no angel-throne, no grace atones, the wind's
wind blown, this one's un-clanned, this one's alone.

After You Die

When it does more to nothing, I let down. I loosen my head and stop arranging my face. Flowers stain my eyelids, red ones and some with leaves like green guitars.

No one says so, but sleeping is TV. Is magical. Flowers strum dark windows. Geraniums and trumpet vines. Amaryllis and belladonna. The shiny petals are dreaming they're scars. Oh, my love, I ride this pleasant moment, no hands, downhill into the quarry.

Me and Virginia

At first I thought they were hieroglyphs. Or tiny cave paintings — but they were marks made by fish bones, Virginia. Lines laid down when oceans covered the Rimrocks. It makes you think, and I'm a fan of thinking. It helps me stay in the room.

Books help too, but last week a student complained about yours. He said Clarissa just confused him, said he likes explicit insight, something with sharp edges that he can talk about at parties. He was unhappy, Virginia, but what he did admire, and he said this twice, was the way you didn't falter at the end. He meant the way you lifted one stone, then another, a frugal housewife, filling your pockets as you headed for the river.

How-to For the Daughters of Suicides

First of all. Be Fine. They want you to. Fix your face, brush your hair, say *I'm fine, thanks, fine.* And in a way, it's true. Because now you don't care what you eat, when you eat, if you eat. You don't care how you look. Or what you think. You don't think. And that's weirdly swell. Like lidocaine. Or being made of chrome.

Tomorrow a long dark car will take you to the cemetery. Wear a plain black dress, or dark blue if you only have that. Later, you must contend with the women who bring casseroles, but otherwise you can relax. Remember, the body must inhabit this space, but there's nowhere your mind has to be.

Lucky So Far

You know what I mean: every summer's the same until it's not. A sore knee here, a twinge there, then one day... slippage. Something loosens. A new reality paints its taste in your mouth. Then it's goodbye to your gung-ho aspiration for the golden moment when you're stronger, faster, smarter. Goodbye to all that.

You start counting. Friends, lovers, books, awards — some days even grandchildren. You find yourself taking longer walks, to the drugstore, to the ice cream shop, maybe even the farmer's market. You wave to strangers with their rescue dogs.

Constable's Landscape

Today the sun's just a stain on winter's sky. The road I've spent a lifetime painting has dipped into the mud and is about to snake itself right out of the frame. There're still a few anorexic trees and a smudge of smoke distorting the heavens, but clearly the painter's ready to clean his brushes. I can't be blamed for a few misgivings.

Descending, even Jonah counted teeth, but dear self, tragedy's a clock that swallows its own ticking. Let's don't be a bore. The next is ever busy becoming the next, and if you stop a moment, that's interesting. Look over there. A white hare is sitting on the snow.

Meditation

The brain balances like broccoli on its stem asking *whose line is it anyway?* We sink into the sofa, still dreaming of chocolate and wine. But the voice says *surrender takes practice.* So we must try. We must practice not knowing. Not meaning. And later we'll speak warily of fire escapes and of our bodies, these shacks at the edge of the swamp.

Dim mirror. Tarnished mirror. Mirror that was once a lake...when Turner painted light on water, he was thinking of us.

In Case of Sudden Free Fall

You can put it in your pocket, in your tire well, in your armpit. You can stash it under your baseball cap, or wrap it up in a handkerchief. You can stuff it in your underwear or hide it in your brand new pigskin wallet. You can slip it under your armband, or bury it in the desert, or whisper it into your cell phone. You can smooth it out and cut it up with little scissors. Or you can fold it. Carefully. Like money.

How Not to Tell a Story

Four men say they saw her, a woman flying. *Her hair was black*, they claim, not softened by brown, nothing to soften the sight of a woman aloft and lit by sun. Her face was burnished *so she must be a saint*, they whisper, *or maybe a sorceress*. Then they re-paint the scene, describing the way she leered, that roof-top woman, her hair now wildly red, uncovered and so red, so bold as she rose to the balls of her feet. As she leaned into sky.

We were struck dumb, they tell us, *by the sight of her* and now they are hissing, *that woman, that witch. She chose to fly*, they mutter, to flee, to fall. She fell. In the market other men take up the story, Eve's daughter, flying to her other life, her after life, human perhaps, but flying. Which, they say, justified the ground that took her like a rough lover.

When They Died

my mom said *heaven* so I knew that in the room of the sky my sisters were jumping rope. One was eight. One was ten, and I wanted to join them, to match their movements, but somehow I'd lived. I'd missed my chance at the room of the heavens.

Every night their wispy silhouettes appeared at the foot of my bed decked out in shine and feathers. Their hands made welcoming gestures. Their throats made song. But I was so sleepy — and too-breathy, too-body, too-heartbeat to follow.

In Praise of What Remains Unfinished

In the last place what you see will be your own — maybe a girl jumping rope or a deer alive and deep in the silvery cottonwoods. So relax. You won't need to justify your life or try to name whatever motors this world. You'll be free to float between attention and daydream, letting your arms feel their elbowy jointedness.

You'll strip off the hair shirt of intellect and notice that what you once called destiny is simply life, the days you slip through till you pull yourself over that last ridge and give up saying *No*. Maybe the sandstone will be hot that day, or maybe there will be rain. Maybe you'll be thinking of Istanbul and your last unfinished project —